MAKE CASH

in INDEPENDENT

TRUCKING

A STEP BY STEP SELF-EMPLOYMENT GUIDE

BRAD WILLIAMS

Copyright

All Rights Reserved. No part of this publication may be reproduced in any form or by any means, without written permission of author. Copyright © 2014
ISBN 978-1-312-56632-3

Disclaimer

This book was written by the author to relay various methods used by successful entrepreneurs in the logistic industry. It is for educational purposes only and written to be as accurate and current as possible. However, rules and regulations do change so this book should not be your ultimate source of information but, rather, a guide. The author makes no guarantees that the methods and tips in this book will work for you, and is not liable for any loss the reader incurs when trying to implement the techniques written in this book.

If....

If you can keep your head when all about you
Are losing theirs and blaming it on you,
If you can trust yourself when all men doubt you,
But make allowance for their doubting too;
If you can wait and not be tired by waiting,
Or being lied about, don't deal in lies,
Or being hated, don't give way to hating,
And yet don't look too good, nor talk too wise:

If you can dream—and not make dreams your master;
If you can think—and not make thoughts your aim;
If you can meet with Triumph and Disaster
And treat those two impostors just the same;
If you can bear to hear the truth you've spoken
Twisted by knaves to make a trap for fools,
Or watch the things you gave your life to, broken,
And stoop and build 'em up with worn-out tools:

If you can make one heap of all your winnings
And risk it on one turn of pitch-and-toss,
And lose, and start again at your beginnings
And never breathe a word about your loss;
If you can force your heart and nerve and sinew
To serve your turn long after they are gone,
And so hold on when there is nothing in you
Except the Will which says to them: 'Hold on!'

If you can talk with crowds and keep your virtue,
Or walk with Kings—nor lose the common touch,
If neither foes nor loving friends can hurt you,
If all men count with you, but none too much;
If you can fill the unforgiving minute
With sixty seconds' worth of distance run,
Yours is the Earth and everything that's in it,
And—which is more—you'll be a Man, my son!

By Rudyard Kipling

Section Content

Section 1: Do I Need a Commercial Driver's License (CDL)?   Page 1

Section 2: Employee vs. Independent Contractor (IC)   Page 4

Section 3: Trucks: Lease or Buy? And Where?   Page 11

Section 4: Insurance: What Type and FMCSA Compliance   Page 14

Section 5: Retail Delivery   Page 16

Section 6: Appliance and Home Delivery   Page 21

Section 7: Bulk Parcel Delivery   Page 26

Section 8: A Word On The Busy Season   Page 28

Section 9: Maintenance   Page 30

Section 10: Employees   Page 32

Make Cash In Independent Trucking: A Step By Step Self-Employment Guide

Foreword

Make Cash In Independent Trucking: A Step By Step Self-Employment Guide is a book based on the collected knowledge and experience of almost 20 years in a variety of transportation niches. It is my hope that it gives usable insight into some areas of the logistic field, and allows you to implement a strategy to overcome obstacles before you reach them. By the end of this book, you should have all the requisite knowledge to start your Independent Trucking business.

The tone of this book was kept light and to the point in the effort to make it easy to read and understand. It is, after all, intended to convey real actions you can take immediately. I'd rather you spend the time implementing the strategies rather than reading a long technical book.

I know your time and resources have value, and I thank you for spending them with me.

Brad Williams

Section 1

Do I need a Commercial Driver's License (CDL)?

The answer to this question depends on what you're hauling and how much of it. You need a CDL if:

- If you are hauling more than 26,000 Gross Vehicle Weight (GVW). This is the combined weight of your truck and your cargo.

- Transporting more than 16 passengers or driving a school bus.

- Your vehicle is specialized: Air Brakes, Transport Tank, Double or Triple trailer.

- You are hauling hazardous materials.

Pretty straight forward. I'll just add that the more endorsements you need, the more it may cost you for your CDL, not including the road tests required for certain endorsements. Also, you must be at least 21 years old, according to the Department of Transportation. Some states allow you to apply at 18, in which case, the CDL is good only in that state.

There are lots of driving schools out there. If you feel like the classroom setting and hands-on instruction is the way for you to get your CDL, then they are fine ways to go about it. However, this can cost thousands of dollars.

The good news is you can acquire your CDL using your own resources. This way will be more complicated for some, but will save you those thousands of dollars. Still be prepared to spend several hundred dollars though.

Start by getting your state's CDL material online or from your local Department of Motor Vehicles. You can study this material on your own and take the written exams yourself. It is definitely intimidating, especially when you have your hard earned money hinging on whether you pass or fail. However, it is possible just by reading and going over the materials until you grasp the concept. Grasping the concept is a very important point; you must do more than just memorize the questions. In the exam, questions will be phrased differently and could even be trick questions. If you have a real understanding of how to apply the knowledge you have read, it will serve you in the written exams as well as the road tests. You will pass the written exams easily because you took the time to invest in yourself, and not too many things will boost your confidence more than knowing your stuff. I will emphasize again, do not just memorize the practice questions at the end of the chapters, the exam questions will almost always be different.

Once you pass the written exams, you will get a learner's permit. Just like when you were a teenager, this means you can drive whatever vehicle you are endorsed for, as long as you have a properly licensed operator with you.

The real challenge comes when you have to find a way to get driving time in the vehicle type you want to take your road test in. Obviously, if you have a friend or family member who can help you with this, it would be great. Most of you won't have that luxury. I would suggest posting your specific needs on craigslist in the transport sections. This is where your hundreds of dollars are going to come into play. You may need to rent a vehicle, and you will also need to pay your newfound instructor for his or her time.

This is truly a much more roundabout way of getting your CDL, but it should still save you thousands of dollars as opposed to going to a driving school. Let's be clear, you will not have the dozens of hours of instructed road time and the professional driving curriculum of a driving school. These are indeed valuable assets, but aren't always affordable for everyone. Therefore, this is a way to outline getting your CDL within your budget. At the end of the day, successful driving comes down to safety first, focus, and good judgment. Exercise these qualities at all times and you will be fine.

Section 2

Employee vs. Independent Contractor (IC).

When you begin to survey the employment opportunities available in the logistic industries, you will notice the descriptions will specify whether they are looking for employees or IC's. Usually, it is more favorable for a company to hire a Delivery Driver as an IC, because they are able to pass expenses such as health insurance and workers compensation on to you. At the same time, they can construct a contract that basically makes you conform to the criteria of an employee. If that is not enough, a company that has hired you as an IC enjoys broad latitude in terms of if or when it wants to terminate your contract. This leaves you out in the cold in regard to any severance or unemployment. We will touch on protecting yourself from these circumstances later.

If you are asking yourself, "Why become an IC? It sounds scary!" Well… you're right, it is scary. It is a horrible feeling to get up for work and get a message that you have been laid off because it's slow. Or maybe you have been fired for some infraction, something as minor as you aren't available to work Saturdays because of your kid's Pee Wee Football games. With that being said, working as an Independent Contractor can provide some excellent opportunities to people who are willing to "pay their dues".

What I mean exactly is, it will take time, hard work, and good judgment to build your business in this field, all while being susceptible to fuel prices, finicky consumers, and managers.

Odds are, if you are reading this, hard work is not scary to you and good judgment often comes with experience. Maybe some of you have time in already, maybe not. But there is one deciding factor in your success in this business. This will be the difference between the person who is going to the poor house between contracts and the person who is able to get another truck, maybe two trucks, out there making money.

Get ready for a clichéd, but truthful answer.

You!

Don't worry, I'll elaborate.

You are the only person responsible for signing an exploitive, restrictive contract. Before signing anything, you have to ask yourself, "What do I want to gain from this?"

If the answer is a decent wage, experience, and physical exercise, then you can be more liberal in what you are willing to accept from a company's contract. Maybe you should even consider going the employee route. You get all of the above, plus benefits, retirement, and further education subsidies.

But if your answers are a little more complex and are along the lines of "I want to make my own schedule", "I want to expand my business within a company's infrastructure", or maybe, "I ultimately want to get out of the truck and manage my business from a desk", then these aspirations mean being more selective in your approach to contracting. The point is, when you sign a contract with a company, you are agreeing to perform a service for them.

Think of yourself as a carpenter or electrician. Would one of those professionals allow their customer to lean over their shoulder and say "Stick that wire in there."? Maybe some would. But the best tradesmen wouldn't hear of it. As long as you are following the contract you have read and signed, use the same broad latitude that the company enjoys to run your business the best you can.

To outline this point in a usable reference, let's use the example of a contract that doesn't specifically prohibit an IC from hiring drivers. You may find that the company may frown upon you hiring employees. They may take that stance because this exact situation turned sour for them in the past or maybe the precedent hasn't been set yet and it threatens the "business as usual" mindset. Nevertheless, as an IC, you cannot be forced to deviate from how you operate your business because of how a company "feels" about something. If a Non Hiring clause isn't part of the agreement you signed with them, there should be no reason you aren't allowed to do so, as long as you are willing to accept the cost associated with your employees hiring. In a nutshell, you must be willing to differentiate their policy from their preference. You, without a doubt, must be willing to stand your ground and use the contract language as a reference to get what you want in your situation. This can come across as aggressive, but it is what you must be willing to do to succeed here. That being said, always remaining professional and using tactful conversation will get you much further should any problems like these arise.

Okay, so now you have submitted a resume to a company and they express enough interest in you to offer a contract. Don't speed read it and sign it on the spot because you're eager to get to work. Take it home and read it carefully. One clue that a company could be undesirable and looking for a wage slave is if they rush you to sign on the spot. This also could mean they have had a person quit or had to fire someone and now need a body to plug in. It may hint at a company with a high turnover.

Read the contract thoroughly and **WRITE DOWN** all questions about anything that concerns or confuses you. These contracts are written by lawyers, so don't be ashamed or scared to ask for clarification. They often detail what exactly is expected from you. For example, a contract may read as:

Independent Contractor compensation

The contractor agrees that in exchange for a day's wage of $269.00, they will provide 8 hours of service as detailed in "paragraph C". These 8 hours do not include travel time to and from the IC's place of business. In addition, Independent Contractors will receive a fuel surcharge that will come into effect based on mileage using current cost per gallon information on a nationwide average.

So in your first read, it may come across as a decent daily wage for an IC. However, in a circumstance like this, where it is worded to the effect that you owe the company 8 hours a day, you may want to question such language. Does it mean that after you evade traffic, catch all green lights, hustle and finish your whole route in 4 hours, you can call it a day and head home? Or are you expected to come back and run again for 4 additional hours to make 8? The expectations can change from company to company or even from driver to driver because of favoritism.

Write any questions like this down and hash them out before you sign the contract. Even ask for an addendum to be added to your contract detailing any concessions or promises made to you during the hiring process. It will not always be granted, but it doesn't hurt to ask. The response you receive after following the above suggestions, may give you some insight into the type of people you will be dealing with. Rational people shouldn't be upset if you ask for some protection for yourself in a contract. Especially because it is written to favor and protect them mostly.

As a side note, there is often no way to avoid paying your dues in jobs like these. You more than likely will be getting the tough runs, and difficult areas to deliver to (i.e., far out runs and congested one way city streets). Most times, the other guys in the warehouse started in the same place. It is one way dispatch can evaluate your performance and tenacity. For a while, just work hard and keep your head down, dot your I's and cross your T's. It will pay off when there is a better opportunity and you decide then to be vocal about wanting a change. By then, you should have proven yourself an asset to them and they will be willing to make some concessions to keep you. If you've been a "good soldier" for a while and have voiced a desire for a better route and still aren't given better opportunities, you may consider a different contract. If you find one, you may be able to use it as leverage in your existing contract.

IMPORTANT

In the above text, I mentioned protecting yourself from loss of income in the event of contract termination. My suggestion is to incorporate your business. You will need to hire a lawyer and set up a corporation through the state you live in. This process usually costs a couple hundred dollars. This is beneficial to you because it protects your personal assets from lawsuits, exposing only your business assets. It also will allow you to work for your own corporation as an employee. What this allows you to do is pay into your state's unemployment pool as a corporation based on the wages you pay yourself. Should the time come when you find that your contract is terminated, you then can collect unemployment as an out of work employee of your own corporation. The benefit of this cannot be overstated as you will at least have some income coming in while you look for a new contract. This should be easy enough, though laws may vary from state to state. One other note is that states usually have a minimum amount that you must earn with a company before you are eligible for unemployment compensation. Read your state's legislation carefully.

In summary, here are some of the Pros and Cons of being an IC.

Pros

- Higher salary

- Self Employed, the business is yours. You are free to hire people to work for your business. You are responsible for managing your business as you see fit. Keep in mind that you must be in compliance with federal and local laws and the language of the contract you have signed.

- Your business related expenses are tax deductible.

- With hard work, sacrifice, and diligence, it is possible to build your business infrastructure inside of a company that hires IC's. This means that you may eventually hire enough drivers and put enough trucks on the road where you can have the option to not work a truck yourself.

Cons

- All expenses are your own. For example: Truck payments, Insurance (Some companies will help with this, as often, one million dollar policies are required. Remember, they are a delivery company, not an insurance company so you will pay a premium for the service.), Registration Fees, Tools and Equipment, Wages for all employees plus their Insurance, Workers Comp, Fuel, Tolls, Paperwork Fees, Drug Testing Fees, Traffic Infraction Penalties, Uniforms, DOT Medical Exams and Repairs, all come out of your pocket.

- As an IC, you have very little protection from arbitrary termination. This means that you can be let go for almost any reason. It is hard to prove if it is a legitimate reason or not. Think about the fact that the contract you sign is drafted by the company you wish to work for. The language of the contract is going to favor them in this regard.

- You will automatically be paying more taxes. You will be paying self-employment tax. Also, if you incorporate (and you should, as this will protect your personal assets in the event your business were to ever get sued), your state may determine you owe a minimum corporate tax, which is due every year, regardless of whether or not your corporation made any profit. Obviously, the more money, the higher the tax.

- Stress. For some, it may be stressful to stay on top of all the aspects of being self-employed on top of the 8 - 10 hours a day of manual labor.

There are more pros and more cons but these are the major ones to consider before you embark on the journey to build a successful trucking business.

Section 3

Trucks: Lease or Buy? And Where?

It goes without saying that your truck is your business's most important asset. It is your primary money maker. The size and year of your truck can even determine how lucrative of a contract you can be offered. Many companies will not offer a contract to an IC if their truck is older than 7 years, for example.

So if you're just starting out and you need a truck, how do you determine whether it's better to lease or buy? Well, let's start with the cold hard facts first. Leasing is probably going to cost you double per month than what buying is going to cost you. A lease contract is usually going to cost between 1000-1600 dollars a month or more, including mileage. Don't forget, that doesn't include fuel. To be clear, the type of lease I am referring to is the rental type offered by companies like Penske and Ryder.

Now, leasing does have its advantages:

- You have no responsibility to fix a leased truck. Beyond routinely checking fluid levels at each fueling and your daily walk around inspection, you are only responsible for repairs if they are the result of your own negligence. Meaning, plug your trucks in when the temperature is below freezing, use anti-gel in the winter, and regularly check your fluid levels. Finally, if you are driving and you hear something amiss, don't drive until you break down, take it in for service.

- No down time. They will swap you out another truck until yours is fixed. They will either bring another truck to your location, where you can swap out your cargo, or bring you to the nearest yard where you can swap out there.

- If you're on a month to month lease, and you are laid off, it really stinks but you're not on the hook for a truck payment. Just turn it back in to the leasing company.

    IMPORTANT NOTE: This is not the case for a long term lease. A long term lease will have cheaper rates, but you will be on the hook for some type of fee if you choose, or are forced, to terminate the lease early.

- New trucks. Usually, the leasing companies buy new instead of fixing up old trucks. This means that you will enjoy newer trucks, if you find that is important to you.

- Insurance can work differently. You may have to have your own, or you may be able to use your job's motor carrier insurance along with using their placards, motor carrier, and DOT numbers. This can save you some money.

This type of leasing works more like a rental program. You can get trucks like this through big outfits like Ryder, Penske, and Budget. There should also be smaller local places in your area as well. Call around and get quotes and use them to leverage the best deal. This is not an ideal long term strategy to build your business. It just costs a lot of money to operate this way, but to get a start in this field, or to save up some money to buy, it would be acceptable.

These lease programs are not to be confused with the dozens of Lease-to-Buy programs out there. These can be disastrous to someone starting out in the delivery business. Many are predatory and designed to milk tons of money out of your business, and then, when an inevitable pitfall happens, they will come and take your truck away. Personally speaking, beyond servicing people who may have damaged credit, they offer no advantage over trying to buy your truck through a financial institution.

There is a no shame in getting your credit dinged up these days, just be very careful and read the fine print if you feel like you're ready to buy and Lease to Buy is your only option.

Maybe you feel like buying a truck right out of the gate is the way to go. If you're in the financial position to do this, then it can be worthwhile. A new 26' straight truck, with a box and liftgate, will probably be 60 to 70 thousand dollars. Assuming you put 25% down, your payment will be in the neighborhood of 800 to 900 dollars a month. Don't forget to factor in insurance.

Buying new just isn't possible for most people, so that leaves buying used. Buying a used truck with less than 200,000 miles can still cost a pretty penny. However, a properly maintained diesel truck can run without any major issues for another 200,000 miles. When buying a used truck, make sure to view a copy of its service records so you can make sure it received a proper preventative maintenance schedule.

To that end, you may consider companies like Ryder that often sell their used fleet maintained trucks. Also, the companies selling trucks may offer an aftermarket warranty; these can also be a good investment.

Getting a good reliable truck out of the gate is very important, downtime for repairs on an unreliable truck cost you money. Too much downtime fixing up a truck can scuttle your business before you get started.

Section 4

Insurance, What Type and FMCSA Compliance.

Insurance for your truck and business can be expensive. The requirements for insurance have a minimum mandated by the FMCSA (Federal Motor Carrier Safety Administration) but your particular employer may want you to carry a policy that exceeds that.

The nuances for insurance are exhaustive and pretty boring. So I will spare you the details in the spirit of keeping this book educational, yet easy to read. I can relay an idea or two about trying to save some money, as I'm sure that is on the forefront on your mind. The more you can save on expenses, the greater the profit margin for your business. I strongly suggest you do your deeper research for insurance requirements at http://www.fmcsa.dot.gov. This website has all the information and resources you need. Read it thoroughly to know what type of insurance to get for what you are hauling, as well as filing for your DOT (Department of Transportation) Number and Motor Carrier Number, if you need them.

One way to save money on insurance and FMCSA fees is by finding a contract that will allow you to use the contracting company's DOT numbers and Motor Carrier Number. The way this works is, basically, when you have their cargo in your vehicle, or are working in some capacity for them, you are under their insurance and their driving authority. You would then only be liable for supplemental insurance for the purpose of driving your truck to or from home or your place of business. This will save you hundreds of dollars a month. The type of insurance for this instance is called Non Trucking Liability Coverage. One of the best resources for this is an organization called NAIT (National Association of Independent Truckers) at http://www.naitusa.com/.

Also, it is possible to tailor your delivery business and contracts so that you may not need DOT numbers or MC numbers. DOT numbers are required federally for Interstate commerce. If your contract doesn't require you to leave the state, then you may not need DOT or MC numbers, saving you hundreds of dollars a year. Most states require you to have DOT numbers, regardless of whether you engage in Interstate commerce or not. Once again, be sure to thoroughly read your state and federal requirements at http://www.fmcsa.dot.gov.

You really don't want to tangle with the DOT. I suggest you don't try to cut any corners. Make sure that your paperwork and driving authorities are bulletproof when you are on the road.

One zealous DOT state trooper can put you out of service on the spot.

To be self-employed, you will have to provide workers' compensation for yourself and any employees you may have. The National Association of Independent Truckers at http://www.naitusa.com/ is a resource for this, as well as other tools for the IC.

Section 5

Retail Delivery

Retail Delivery

If you are just starting out in retail delivery, here are some tools, tips, and terms to make your life easier.

If you have been delivering retail for years....read it anyway, maybe there is a perspective you haven't heard before.

The Lowdown on Retail Delivery

Retail Delivery, in most cases, is labor intensive and demanding. It usually involves working as an independent contractor or employee of a logistic provider. The logistics provider, in turn, contracts with the actual retail stores or parent company of several retail stores. To get these very lucrative contracts, the logistic provider generally agrees to contract language basically guaranteeing that they will operate in the 95th percentile or above in several categories, some of which are: On time deliveries, Shrinkage (theft, damage, etc…), and performance levels. If the company falls short, needless to say, they lose the business, maybe at the end of the contract, or, depending on the contract structure, immediately. This ultimately creates a high pressure and demanding work environment. The delivery person walking into a workplace such as this can expect organized chaos in the best case, and a complete calamity in the worst.

Delivery drivers are expected to get their truckloads delivered on time and intact, regardless of all circumstances except the most extenuating. More than likely, you will see a bunch of other delivery drivers rushing around trying to get loaded and on the road. Don't worry about them, be respectful and courteous but don't be a pushover. Their loads don't take precedent over yours (unless a supervisor makes it known to you, and even then, question it.)

This is a very brief description of the Retail Delivery business at the delivery person level. Below are some tools, tips, and terms necessary to be successful.

Tools, Tips, and Terms

Terms

- Manifest – This should be the first thing you want to find and read. It should have all essential information about the day's load. The who, what, where, and how much. Any questions or confusion, ASK! Do not assume or guess, especially if you're concerned that the weight may exceed your GVW (Gross Vehicle Weight).

- Pallets – This is the raised wood or plastic platform that freight is often staged on for ease of movement. It is also called a skid. A 26' foot box can usually fit 12 pallets straight in, and more, if some are turned sideways.

- Pallet jack - Hand powered jack for moving pallets.

- Two Wheeler - Two wheeled cart for moving a stack of boxes. It is also called a dolly.

- Shrink wrap – Plastic wrap on a roll used to secure loose freight staged on a pallet.

- DOT – Department of Transportation. State troopers trained and authorized to pull over commercial vehicle at any time to inspect for safety and weight compliance. This is serious business if you find you have to travel in or through states like Connecticut, Maine, Missouri, or the Carolinas.

- LTL – Less than truckload shipping.

- Load Bar – A bar used for securing freight inside of the truck. These should always be utilized. And DOT does look for them upon inspection.

- Load Strap – Same purpose as a load bar except a strap with various end types for fasten points.

- E-Track System - This is a fastening system that is sometimes used in the box of a truck. It has specialized clips and straps.

Tools
- Marker/Sharpie
- Pallet Jack
- Two Wheeler
- Shrink Wrap
- Load Bars
- Load Straps
- Door Chocks
- Camera phone or Camera

Tips
- Read your entire manifest; take note of any pickups and their count. You obviously can't do a large pickup as your first stop because it will force you to work around it the rest of the day.

- Take note of delivery windows (Times the store will accept deliveries). The manifest may be ordered in a way to take advantage of this already. If not, you will have to number them yourself. If all the deliveries have the same windows, or do not have delivery windows (Lucky!), number the stops in an order that will prevent you from having to backtrack or zigzag, if possible.

- Now that you have gone over your manifest and numbered your deliveries in order, you are ready to walk the floor. Your manifest should indicate in some way the location of each of your deliveries.

Find them and verify the count if they are not already shrink-wrapped. Mark the count on the skid with a marker while also marking the pallet count for example: "36 pieces skid 1 of 2 or skid 1/2." Counting your freight is important if it is part of your job description because somewhere along the line, you will have to sign your name for it, and that means you are responsible for anything missing. This includes any freight you notice that is damaged or open. Bring it to dispatch's attention and have them initial your manifest to verify. Some of them may gripe at you, but it is better than you being left holding the bag.

- Now that you have wrapped and counted your freight, you are ready to load. You want to load your truck in reverse order of your numbered manifest! I cannot tell you how many new guys I have seen load their entire truck backwards. Your last stop should be loaded first.

- Write or engrave your name or company name on all of your equipment. Theft of your equipment is costly and enraging.

- If you have a pull down style door on your truck, slack can build up in the door system, causing your door to hang a few inches lower than the threshold when open. An easy fix is to use a slim door chock or a broken pallet splinter to prop it open all the way. Wedge it into the door track behind the last door runner.

- If you have secured your freight properly using a load bar or strap, the cargo should withstand the rigors of driving. It will be upright and in good condition when you arrive at your first stop. Remember to secure it again when you leave to your next delivery.

- This tip is probably one of the most important, so pay attention. The most valuable tool you have in your toolbox is a good relationship with the receiver in the store or warehouse you are delivering to. Be respectful and courteous but don't be a pushover, just like in the home terminal. Engage them and use their name while introducing yourself by your own. Make them see you as a person, not a tool.

Try to accommodate them without sacrificing your own delivery schedule or doing their job for them. One day, the-you-know-what will hit the fan, but if the receiver is in your corner, it can go a long way in making things right. That being said, there are some seriously miserable people out there and they will be impossible to deal with. In these occasions, I can only relate my own actions, which were: let them know courteously that you are one tree they don't want to bark up, then ignore them completely while trying to get your job done if possible. In cases where you have some type of difficulty, call your dispatcher as soon as possible and notify them of any potential complaints. The dispatcher will enjoy a little heads up and be more appreciative hearing about it from you first.

- If anything unusual happens, or some circumstance prevents you from completing your task in full, take pictures along with calling dispatch as soon as possible. Obviously, the pictures back up what you're saying and calling dispatch will put the onus on them on how to proceed from that point. That's what they are paid for. Never jeopardize your safety or anyone else's to make a delivery. In the end, it's just stuff, they'll make more. Protect your truck the same way.

    Note: After making that point, if there is an opportunity to go the "extra mile" safely for a worthy dispatcher, do it. It will pay off down the road.

That, in a nutshell, should cover the basics of retail delivery. Good luck and challenge yourself to be the best.

Section 6

Appliance and Home Delivery

<u>Appliance/Home Delivery</u>

Trying to get your foot in the door as an appliance or home delivery team? Here are some tools, tips, and terms to give you a head start.

<u>The Scoop on Appliance/Home Delivery</u>

Appliance Delivery has a lot of similarities to Retail Delivery. This field shares the tendencies to hire Independent Contractors, but there are many retail stores that hire employees to do this work as well. It is also labor intensive and, frankly, more demanding than Retail Delivery as you are servicing a consumer in their home. This means that, often times, you will be expected to work Saturdays and even Sundays as that is often the time when people are home to receive a delivery.

These contracts also tend to demand more technical ability as you will be doing light to moderate installs of appliances such as things like washers and dryers and water lines for refrigerators.

Home Delivery is very similar; a lot of companies hire IC's to deliver consumer goods like patio sets and fitness equipment. In either contract scenario, you will have to have a full assortment of tools to get the various jobs done.

Operations that facilitate appliance and home deliveries are companies that distribute for a large, or even nationwide, retailer. They then search for IC's to make the last mile delivery and installation.

Here are some of the Pros and Cons of a contract like this.

Pros:
- More pay. Delivering and installing appliances will earn as much as $30 - $40 per stop. With some routes having more than 20 stops, you can see the payout potential. Home delivery of other product goods can pay as much as $300 a stop, depending on the complexity of the install. An example of a $200 - $300 home delivery is an in ground basketball hoop.

Cons
- This is always a two man job; as such, you will depend on another person. Make sure they are reliable. I cannot stress that enough.
- Work seven days a week, including most holidays. This business is centered on accommodating customers when they are home. So it goes without saying that they are home on the weekends. Dispatch will give you days off by law, but they are often irregular.

Tools, Tips, and Terms

Terms
- No terminology here that you wouldn't be familiar with.

Tools
- GPS
- Fully Outfitted Toolbox
- Marker/Sharpie
- Two Wheeler
- Appliance Dolly
- Electrical Tape
- Water Line Fittings
- Moving Straps (Shoulder Dolly)
- Shrink Wrap

- Load Bars
- Load Straps
- Door Chocks
- Camera phone or Camera

Tips

You're going to load your truck with your last stop going on first. Now, in appliance delivery, you always have to assume that for every piece you take off, there will be one coming back on as a "Haul Away" (Customer's old unit). So that means that when loading all your days stops, they have to be staged in a way that "haul away's" don't get in your way. To do this, load the last stop on the left hand side of your box first. Next, load the second stop to the right of the first. Next, load your third stop to the right of the second. If it doesn't fit there, load it in front of the second stop. Load the fourth stop in front of your third stop. It should start to look like an upside down and inverted L. When you are done loading, you should have a somewhat open space on the left side of your truck for "haul away's". As your deliveries are coming off and "haul away's" are coming on, you will need to rotate the load so your next delivery is always closest to the door, while the "haul away's" are being rotated to the back.

- If your company doesn't supply you with one, you will need to establish a spare parts bin. This will have things in it like dryer feet, washer hoses, range plugs, and dryer vents. Often, the customer orders these things when they buy an appliance, but sometimes a particular item will be omitted from your manifest. You will need to provide it on the spot to keep the customer satisfied. Sometimes, the customer will have bought them separately and have them waiting for you. Note on your manifest if you had to provide something from your bin. If it was an out of pocket expense for you, make sure you are reimbursed.

- Always keep your team in motion. When you are introducing your team to the customers and getting the placement for the item, your helper should be measuring the doorways and clearing obstacles.

When you are doing the closeout and demonstration with the customer, your helper should be picking up any rubbish and checking that all the tools are back in the toolbox. Also, they should be rotating the next delivery and "haul away's".

- Don't use any type of dolly with wheels on a finished floor. Any marks or damage will cost you your day's pay.

- If your truck has a leak of any kind, don't park in the customer's driveway.

- Be careful of plants and flowers when moving appliances to a rear door or bulkhead.

- If you are delivering a lawn tractor, or gas powered machine, give the customer a phone call in advance to find out if they have gas for a closeout demonstration. If they have an old tractor or machine for you to haul away, make sure it is empty of fuel.

- It may go without saying but I'll say it anyway. Under no circumstance take a "haul away" that has evidence of roaches or other pest infestation. You run the risk of spreading the infestation to other customers or your own home.

- Almost all jobs like this will get a follow up phone survey from the parent company. The point of the survey is to evaluate your delivery. To ensure good surveys, be frank with the customer. Ask them "Is there any reason that you would say I deserve less than a top score on a survey? If so, how can I correct it?" It may seem like pandering, and maybe it is, but put yourself in their shoes. If you had just shelled out big bucks for an item, wouldn't it make you feel better to know that your delivery person was trying to make you happy? That being said, some customers are impossible to please and in that case, you just have to get out as soon as possible.

- Have your helper learn how to interact with the customers. This is great for times when you're in no mood to be Mr. Nice Guy. If your helper can handle all aspects of the job, he is your first potential candidate to put into another truck as a driver.

These are some really good starter points to give you a head start in the appliance/home delivery field. Get out there and make some money!

Section 7

Bulk Parcel Delivery

<u>Bulk Parcel Delivery</u>

Lucrative opportunities for IC's who can land them, they are in high demand. Be prepared for stiff competition and less than honorable tactics by competitors.

<u>The Real Deal on Bulk Parcel Delivery.</u>

Bulk Parcel Delivery contracts are some of the best available to the Independent Contractor. The reasoning behind this is, unlike many retail locations or a personal residence, your stops will usually be another distribution facility equipped with the space and personnel to receive palletized loads.

To explain it another way, you won't be handling the freight yourself other than loading and unloading pallets. This is much, much less labor intensive, therefore, you are spending less time on the job. Less time on a job that pays you a fixed amount, based on your route, means you are making more per hour, and not doing as much manual labor. There is nothing wrong with manual labor, but over time, repetitive movement injuries like carpal tunnel syndrome and shoulder and knee wear and tear can cause you problems.

The facilities you are delivering to take packages intended for the same destination or area. Once you drop off the pallet, it is broken down and items are delivered directly to individual addresses.

A good example of this type of operation is the service, Smartpost. Smartpost parcels are sorted and staged by Fedex. Fedex will hire a logistic company to get the parcels to local Post Offices. The logistic company will hire IC's to do the deliveries to the Post Offices The Post Office will then break down the pallets and deliver them the "Last Mile" to the customer.

Compare that to loading and delivering a truckload of refrigerators, or lumping a hundred boxes from your truck to a storage room in a retail store. You begin to see that these are the type of contracts that you want to keep your eye out for. When one comes available, it is worth your time to try and secure it for your business.

Tools, Tips, and Terms

This type of contract doesn't require much, maybe a pallet jack, if there isn't one to use at the various locations, and load straps or bars, and that's about it. There may be some implementation of electronic scanning or a process of uploading a real time delivery confirmation. If scanning is required, a scanner will be provided to you by the logistic company you contract with, maybe at a charge. Real time delivery confirmation can be done today via cell phone. Getting a phone that is compatible with certain software may be an expense out of your pocket.

All in all, these contracts are about as easy as it gets in the logistic business.

Section 8

A Word On The Busy Season.

If at this point of the book you have said to yourself, "I don't have enough experience to get a contract. I've never even driven a truck before." Then this section can alleviate those concerns. During the busy season, it is all hands on deck for logistic companies and almost all of them are willing to give you a chance, if you're willing to work hard.

The busy season can start in September (Christmas), though sometimes as early as August (Back to School), and usually ends in January some time.

This timeframe is wide open for making some extra cash. The work will almost always exceed the available driver pool. So you and all your drivers will be asked if you are available to work Saturdays, or even do another trip or two. Start planning ahead for this time of year to maximize your profits. Work out your availability as well as the drivers in your employ, and do your preventative maintenance ahead of schedule so you will not experience down-time during peak season.

Peak season means peak car traffic, shoppers, work, and frazzled nerves. It is the holiday shopping season, and stores and consumers will demand goods in large quantities. It will generally be a tough season for the delivery person. It is not unusual to see a driver burn out. The only thing I can suggest is to take a little extra care of yourself during this time. Make sure you get your proper rest and take water, high energy food, and aspirin with you in case you need them.

I can relate a personal experience in this regard.

One peak season, I was asked to cover another person's run because they had injured their back. I agreed because usually this dispatcher looked out for my interests and it's a two way street. The run I covered was far from my home on a normal day, about 90 minutes if traffic wasn't bad. This, however, was peak season and traffic is always bad. Added to that was after finishing in about 9 hours, a flash snowstorm swept down on the region. Now, unexpectedly, it took me 4 and half hours of tense winter driving to get home. My shoulders were tense driving in those conditions after a long work day. I was fortunate to have some aspirin with me. The point of all this is to show you never know when you could be delayed or even stopped by unforeseen circumstances. There were plenty of trucks that got stuck on the highway that night. The chance is higher during peak because of winter conditions and the volume of people out and driving is increased. Be prepared.

That being said, most drivers find that the money flows freely this time of year and count on this period to make a nice chunk of change.

A last note, dozens of ICs and drivers will be hired at this time of year. Dozens will be laid off in January. Be extra careful if you are hanging hopes on a long term contract and you are hired during peak season. Make sure your assurances of long term work are rock solid before you commit a lot of resources or leave another contract to take a new one during peak season.

If you are getting your very first start in the delivery business during peak season, don't be discouraged if you find yourself laid off in January. You have now accumulated some valuable experience in the field's most demanding situation. It is possible to stick even after the slow season starts, if management sees something in you. You can give yourself a higher chance of retention by doing the job well, first and foremost. Secondly, engage dispatchers and upper managers. I do not mean suck up to them, I mean engage them and make them see you as a person with a name, not a breathing body in a truck.

Section 9

Maintenance

This section is to briefly emphasize the importance of a maintenance budget. Many will already grasp this and have the discipline to set aside the necessary assets.

Once you have an established contract, and you find yourself profitable, you must immediately start a maintenance fund. This should be at least 10% of your gross weekly income, rain or shine, per truck. In all honesty, it should be more along the lines of 20%, but for those who struggle to save for a rainy day, 10% is mandatory. So, for the money that *each* truck generates, take 10 - 20% off the top for maintenance.

Every 3000 miles or every three months, whichever comes first, take your truck in for a Preventative Maintenance (PM) appointment. The mechanic will change your oil and filter, grease your fittings, and give your truck a once over inspection. They should be able tell you of any wear and tear issues that may be a problem down the road.

The probability that you will need the money in a maintenance account is 100%. It is a literal guarantee that the day will come where your truck will need some form of maintenance. The where, when, and how is under your control only to a certain degree. Unexpected emergency repairs happen all the time and having money ready to deal with a scenario like that can be the difference in whether your business thrives or sinks.

Here is a scenario:

At your PM appointment, your mechanic tells you are going to need brakes by your next PM. Let's look at the ways this hypothetical situation could play out.

A) You use the allocated 10 - 20% you have saved for this reason and schedule the brake repair. Costly, but you have saved for just such an occasion.

B) You have not saved and decide to get it done when you have the money together. Your brakes become unresponsive in the middle of a route and you cannot safely drive back to your garage. This is extremely costly, because unless you are a mobile mechanic with just the right tools and parts, you now have to call for roadside assistance. It entails either a tow or a repair. These shops could easily get $100 an hour or more, starting from the time they leave to help you. Now you're out a couple of hundred dollars for the roadside assistance, add the brake repair, and add the unscheduled downtime of not having your truck available to work. Plus, the fact that you have no budget for repairs, and your business is in serious trouble and looks like you will be heading to the land of credit card debt.

C) Same as B) except your brake failure causes an accident, all the expenses of the above, except throw in a couple of police citations and insurance claims and... well, hopefully, you get the picture.

Do yourself a *huge* favor and make a maintenance budget and stick to it religiously.

If you really are in a position where you can't afford to allocate resources to a maintenance budget, you have to reevaluate your expenses. If after that, you cannot come to a solution where your business makes a profit and you can save money for future maintenance, then maybe you need a new contract or job altogether. Sometimes, it's like that. The only thing I will reiterate is that it is a "slam dunk" guarantee that your truck is going to need expensive repairs at some point. Wear items, like tires and brakes, alone could be thousands of dollars.

Section 10

Employees

The last section of this book details some tips on managing additional drivers or employees of your business.

More than likely, this will be the perpetual headache of your business. The problems arise from there simply being not enough capital to keep great employees. Everyone wants a "Johnny on the Spot", super responsible, and trustworthy employee, but how can you pay them what their value is?

Think of your business in a pie graph. You will be paying out: Fuel, Maintenance, Insurance, Registration and Equipment costs. By law, you must provide workers compensation as well. That leaves a small slice of the profit for you, which you then must pay an employee from. It's just not much and certainly not enough to keep a great worker who knows his worth for the long term.

You may be asking yourself, "Why even bother to hire someone to drive for me?" The answer is, once you have established a route that can generate money without you, you are free to do something else. You can now drive a second route yourself, until you have saved up enough money to put another truck and driver on the road. One extra route probably won't build your business up to the point where you can get out of a truck. The ability to do that will come with scaling up your operation one route at a time. Let's say, for example, that after all expenses are paid out, your extra route generates $200 profit a week. You obviously can't get out of your truck on that, but if, over the span of a few years, you can scale that up to four or five routes… Well, now you're talking about clearing $800 to $1000 a week.

You will be in a management position and may have to spend your time making sure all drivers and equipment are functioning the way they are supposed to. Don't get too far ahead though; it starts with you establishing one route at a time. It also is vital that you find good, reliable drivers to work your routes, people whose values reflect your own as closely as possible. The problem, as I mentioned earlier, is that those types of people are often expensive.

So what are some ideas to keep him/her around?

First, try lightening their responsibilities. Show up in the mornings and help them load out, show your face, and talk to your drivers. A great and fast load out is a huge jump start to the day. Show up extra early and count, wrap, and stage their freight, so when they show up, all they have to do is grab a door and load. This will go a long way. It also helps you verify the load outs of all your drivers if you counted and staged it yourself, in case a discrepancy is found later in the day.

Another tip comes into play before an employee is even hired. Let's say, after crunching the numbers for your business, you figure out you can put another truck on the road and pay a driver $110 a day to work it. I would suggest you start the hiring process with the promise of $80 a day and after a probation period, they can earn $90. If you feel like a person is a winner and they haggle, offer $100. If they pass probation and start earning the $90-$100, take the $10-$20 difference from your original calculations and save it in a bonus/performance account for each driver.

An example is this:

Bob is working for you for a $100 a day, it is peak season and he is slammed with work. You help him load out, but he is still angry. You can sense it. He heads out and his third stop has no receiver on duty to check in the freight and the store or company won't let him in right away. Now he is fuming because he can't work around what is in the back of his truck to come back to this stop later, so he has to wait there and his wage of $100 a day is turning into $6 an hour at this rate. He makes the call, it sounds like, "Boss, you've been great, helping me in the mornings and all, but this just isn't worth the money or aggravation. I want to give my notice." You respond, "Look, Bob, I know it's a rough one today, but peak is almost over then things will settle down. Will an extra 50 bucks for today's run make this right for you?"

Maybe it will. Maybe it will cost you $100 extra. The point of all of this is the psychological benefit for Bob is invaluable. He is happy because you responded to his problems and tried to fix them. You are happy because you kept a great employee, for what you already had allocated in the performance/bonus account to pay him.

In addition to having money for scenarios like the above, the same performance account can be used to pay a quarterly bonus. For example, every three months a check for $200 - $300 if they hit certain performance markers you set. For example, they have no last minute call outs that quarter, or they never forget freight back at the warehouse. This will also go a long way in keeping quality employees.

Now, let's say a couple of years pass this way and your great employee basically knows everything you know and is ready to get his own contract. The business relationship does not have to end there.

By then, you will know first-hand how tough it will be to just start out. You can still make a profit and help out your former employee as they get their own business started.

How?

Make them an offer to lease the truck they are using. It will work like this. First, consider asking a lawyer to write up a generic truck lease you can use repeatedly. If, or when, your employee wants to get their own contract, offer them a fair lease for about 25% lower than the best offer they get from a leasing or rental company.

It's a win/win scenario. They win because they save money during the initial startup phase of their contract. You win because you can still make money off of your truck. If you feel like you prefer to hire another driver to run the truck, then make an agreement to lease the truck out for a set time of 30-90 days. This gives you plenty of time for hiring someone and keeps your truck working while you are screening potential employees. You could even send out some potential employees on the truck in a probationary period to see how they hold up.

This probably all sounds pretty concise and straightforward, but in reality, there other pitfalls and obstacles. It is my hope that this information as well as the other sections of this book will help you avoid the major ones.

www.ingramcontent.com/pod-product-compliance
Lightning Source LLC
Chambersburg PA
CBHW080852170526
45158CB00009B/2710